Five Nights at Freddy's Drawing Guide

Published by Walter Gutenberg

Table of Contents

Introduction

Hey there, dear FNAF lover!

Welcome to the Five Nights at Freddy's Drawing Guide! Inside, you'll find all the instructions necessary to start creating fabulous masterpieces. Soon enough, you'll be winning awards, having your work showcased in galleries and, if you're extremely lucky, get a place of honor on the fridge. Truly, there is no higher glory.

This first drawing book has been designed with beginners in mind, and aims to carefully show you how to draw each and every project. There are twelve fantastic drawings for you to sketch out with all you amazing talent, so good luck and have fun!

Thanks again for supporting us by purchasing this book. We at Gutenberg Publishing hope you have an awesome time drawing up some scary pictures!

Enjoy!

Five Nights at Freddy's Drawing Guide

Freddy

Step 1:

To start off, make a circle for the head guide then sketch in the facial guidelines in the shape of a "plus symbol". You'll be doing this for most of the drawings, so don't be afraid to practice.

Step 2:

Using the head guide, you can begin drawing the shape and structure of Freddy's head. Add the bumps for the cheeks. Afterwards, make the shape of a muzzle (it kinda looks like an egg), before drawing and coloring a nose.

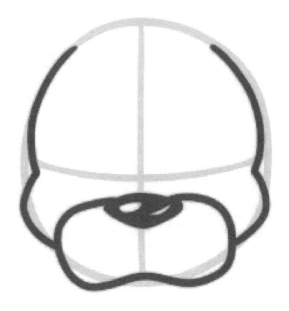

Step 3:

Now for the hat! If you hadn't noticed, Freddy's hat looks like a small layered cake in a very square design. Draw a couple of rectangles on top of each other, then a lid to hold them up.

Step 4:

Now we can draw Freddy's ears. They look like small caps with bolt stems, or windows.

Step 5:

Use the facial guidelines to draw in the thick slightly arched eyebrows like so. They're in the shape of bananas. Then draw the hollows of the eyes. Make the eyeballs (which are pretty much circles) which have eyelids that are half closed.

Step 6:

Finally, draw the bottom jaw, then add four visible square teeth. Add a line for his lip down the center of the face, starting at the base of the nose. Once done, erase any mistakes you might have made (though you're probably too skilled for that).

Step 7:

And there you have it! One awesome drawing of Freddy Fazbear, for you to color in.

Bonnie

Step 1:

Like with Freddy, draw a circle and then sketch in the facial guidelines.

Step 2:

Start off by drawing the structure of Bonnie's head. It kinda resembles a Goomba from Super Mario Brothers. Afterwards, draw the muzzle.

Step 3:

For the nose, draw an egg shape and color it in. Once done, draw the lip line from the nose to the bottom of the muzzle.

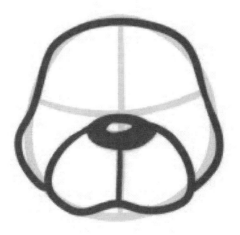

Step 4:

Draw a pair of large eye hollows, then fill them with Bonnie's pupils.

Step 5:

Now for the bottom jaw. This is really easy, just draw a pair of half circles.

Step 6:

Next for the ears! They're like penguin flippers.

Step 7:

Draw a smaller pair of flippers in the ears, then draw a slightly curved line going through the center.

Step 8:

Finally, for the teeth! Would you believe these also look like little flippers? Fill Bonnie's mouth with this gnashers and you're good to go.

Step 9:

And here is the finished product!

Chica

Step 1:

Chica is incredibly easy to draw, considering she doesn't need any facial guidelines. Start off with the outline of her head. Notice it's the shape of an upside down apple.

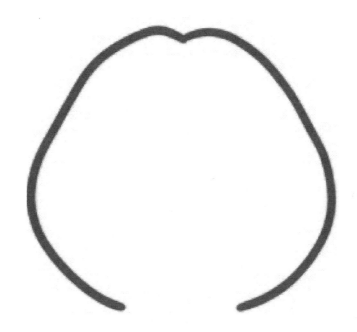

Step 2:

Draw Chica's beak. For the top portion, copy the shape we've drawn below. Then, add a half circle below that.

Step 3:

Add another half circle for the bottom mandible of the beak. Also add a couple of notches on the nose for nose holes.

Step 4:

Draw thick, dark circles for the eye sockets, then draw a dot in both of them for the pupils. Draw and color in the eyebrows (remember, banana shape).

Step 5:

Now for the teeth! Kinda like flippers, similar to what we did with Bonnie. Remember that Chica has quite a few teeth to bite down on her victims. Nom nom nom.

Step 6:

Lastly, draw two small feathers and one big feather on top of her head. Think leaves. Erase any mistakes you might have made and you're done!

Step 7:

Color in if so desired, but otherwise Chica is finished.

Foxy

Step 1:

Draw a circle and facial guidelines like with previous animatronics, but this time add a U shape at the bottom.

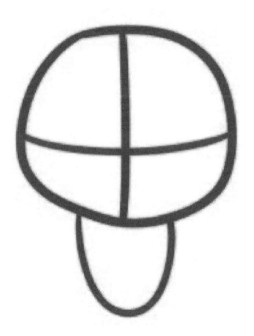

Step 2:

Define the shape of Foxy's head. This is a little tricky, but if you follow the sketch we've drawn below then you should be fine. Don't forget the pointed bits at the side and the feathers on his head.

Step 3:

Draw Foxy's ears (in the shape of spears), and attach them to his head with two small lines. Draw a pair of smaller spear shapes inside his ears as well.

Step 4:

On the left of his face, draw Foxy's eyepatch (two rectangles and a circle, colored in). For his eye, draw a thick eye socket. Draw a line through half of the circle, and add his pupil. Don't forget to do the snout (oval shape).

Step 5:

Add holes for Foxy's whiskers, then draw the nose (egg shape). Leave some tiny nose tips as well, then color the nose in black.

Step 6:

Copy the shape below to draw Foxy's jaw.

Step 7:

Inside the jaw, add a bottom and top row of sharp teeth for Foxy. He needs to eat too. Once done, erase your mistakes and guidelines.

Step 8:

Man that thing looks creepy. Still, enjoy your new Foxy!

Golden Freddy

Step 1:

Draw a circle and sketch in facial guidelines. You should be an expert at this by now.

Step 2:

Draw the shape of Golden Freddy's head, whilst adding bumps for his cheeks.

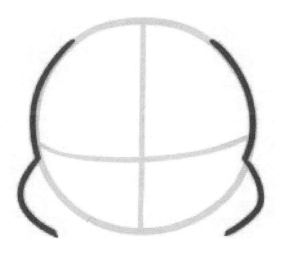

Step 3:

Next up is the muzzle. Copy the shape down below and you should be fine.

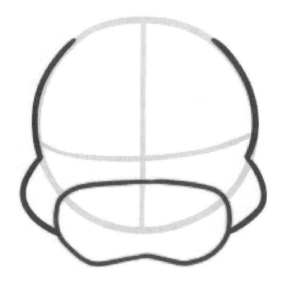

Step 4:

Draw the nose and color it in. Erase a spot on the nose and add some white (for a glare effect). Draw the lip line from nose to muzzle, and add a few scruff marks.

Step 5:

Draw the empty hollows of Golden Freddy's eyes (he has no pupils). Draw the eyebrows (bananas, in a mean expression. Add the wire sticking out from the hollow of the left eye (tip: it looks like bacon strips), then sketch in more scuff marks on the face.

Step 6:

Now for the top hat! Exactly the same as Freddy's, with two rectangles on top of each other, sitting in a lid shape.

Step 7:

Draw Freddy's left ear and add detailing to it (exactly the same as Freddy's). For the right ear, just add wires (bacon) hanging from the hole.

Step 8:

For Golden Freddy's jaw, it's a simple double U (or half circle) shape.

Step 9:

Add ze teeth for ze biting!

Step 10:

FINISHED! Excellent work, if I do say so myself.

Toy Freddy

Step 1:

You know the drill! Circle and facial guidelines.

Step 2:

Draw the shape of Toy Freddy's head, with slight bumps for the cheeks. Add an oval shape for his jaw.

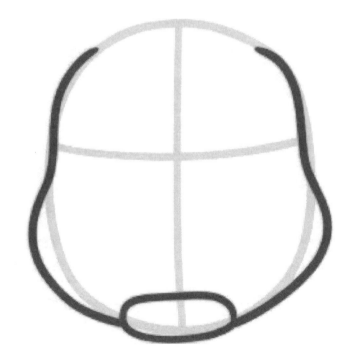

Step 3:

Toy Freddy's hat is a little different to regular Freddy's. Draw a square shape, with a line near the bottom going from left to right. Add a thin rectangle below that.

Step 4:

Draw Toy Freddy's ears! They look like spoons.

Step 5:

Draw the muzzle shape (two half circles), then an oval shape (colored in) for the nose.

Step 6:

Add a few freckles, along with a line down the center of the muzzle. Draw the mouth lines and add some square teeth.

Step 7:

Add some eyebrows (aka bananas). Draw a couple of eye sockets, and erase a tiny portion for the pupils. Add a couple of circles for cheeks. Then, erase the guidelines and any mistakes.

Step 8:

Awww! It's so cute... and very deadly. Be on your guard.

Toy Bonnie

Step 1:

Start off by drawing the head shape. Like with Chica, we don't need any facial guidelines.

Step 2:

Next up is to draw the mouth and nose area. Color in a nose, then make a bottom shape for the lower part of the mouth. In all honesty, it looks like a cupcake with a cherry on top.

Step 3:

Add a U shape for the lip.

Step 4:

Draw and color in the eyebrows (do I need to say what they look like?), then add circles for the cheeks. Don't forget the sharp teeth, hehehe.

Step 5:

Draw a pair of large circles for the eyes, and add a pair of eyelids at the top.

Step 6:

Add another circle around the eyes, then add a few eyelashes. Then add some eyes and pupils, along with some freckles. Finally, add a small line beneath the nose.

Step 7:

Draw Toy Bonnie's ears as shown below.

Step 8:

Draw the exact same shapes inside his ears. Once done, erase the guidelines and mistakes.

Step 9:

We've finished yet another adorable animatronic! Well done!

Toy Chica

Step 1:

Draw a circle. This is probably the most difficult part in the entire book. I know it looks incredibly tough, but just believe in yourself! You can do it! I know you can! Draw the best darn circle in the world!

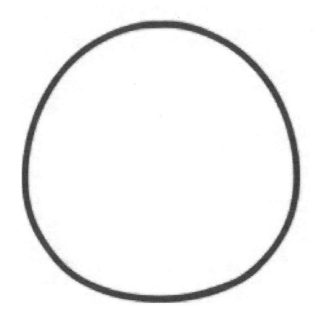

Step 2:

Draw the feathers sprouting from Toy Chica's head.

Step 3:

Draw the hollows of Toy Chica's eyes, whilst adding a little bit of detail at the sides for each eye.

Step 4:

Now draw the beat/mouth! It kind of looks like a bowl, minus the cereal.

Step 5:

So we can transform the the mouth into a beak, add a lip line at the top of the mouth. Then add some lovely teeth!

Step 6:

To finish up, color inside the mouth. Afterwards add some cheek circles and then draw eyebrows/bananas. Don't forget to color in the eyes. Then just erase the mistakes and you're done!

Step 7:

And here you go! One Toy Chica, ready to serve up some pancakes!

Balloon Boy

Step 1:

Circle and guidelines, the usual.

Step 2:

Define the shape of BB's face with a U shape.

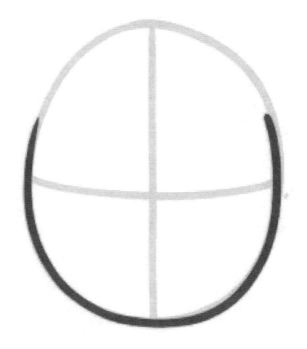

Step 3:

Draw a couple of lines on the side to serve as the ears, then draw Balloon Boy's cap. Essentially a half circle with a little bump.

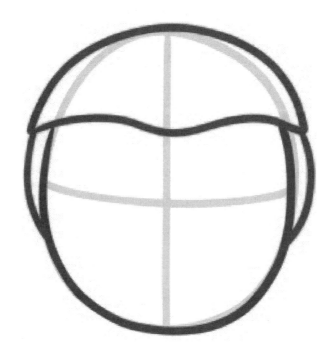

Step 4:

Draw a pair of eyes, complete with eyelids. Afterwards, add a diamond-shaped nose.

Step 5:

Add another circle for the eyes, followed by a pair of irises. Then add circles for the cheeks, along with a tongue and some square teeth. Don't forget the nose line!

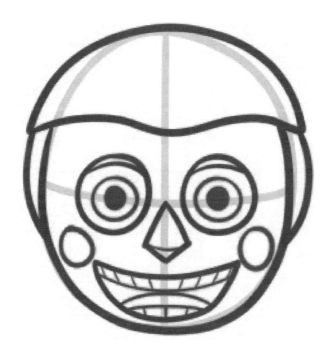

Step 6:

Add some stripes to Balloon Boy's cap.

Step 7:

Finally, add a little button on top of the head, followed by the propeller!

Step 8:

And you're done! Another fantastic image, ready to go.

Mangle

Step 1:

Mangle is very similar to Foxy, so we'll design the guidelines like we did for him. Circle, facial guidelines and a U shape at the bottom.

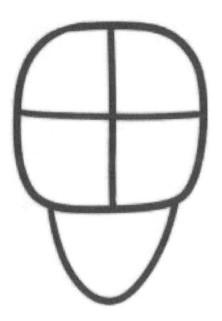

Step 2:

Define the top portion of Mangle head. If you look carefully, it's similar to a hat. Note how it slopes down into two pointed parts.

Step 3:

Add a pair of eyes and a half circle for the muzzle.

Step 4:

Add another circle around the eyes, before adding a pair of eyelids, a pair of eyelashes and one eyeball.

Step 5:

Draw two circles on the cheeks, then add a half circle for the mouth and a triangle for the nose.

Step 6:

Add a pair of smooth ears (again, think flippers), along with Mangle's loose wiring (again, think strips of bacon).

Step 7:

Add some detail to the ~~flippers~~ ears.

Step 8:

Almost done! Draw the shape of Mangle's jaw, as shown below.

Step 9:

Add another loose wire to the left side of his face, along with a circle on the bottom jaw for a bit of detail. Then, slot some nice, sharp teeth in and you're finished.

Step 10:

And voila! Another creepy animatronic for your collection.

The Puppet

Step 1:

Make a lovely circle and some facial guidelines, for what will soon become a very creepy Halloween decoration.

Step 2:

Sketch out the shape of the Puppet's face. Remember to add some prominent cheeks. We want him to look similar to a mask.

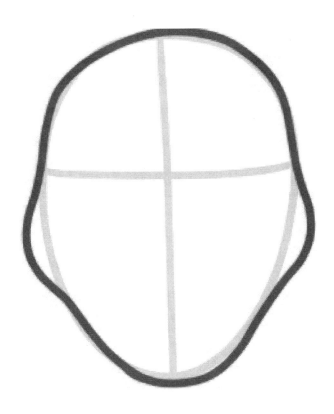

Step 3:

Add the hollows for the eyes and the mouth. Note that the eyes look like flying saucers.

Step 4:

Now we'll add some detail to the face! Add some smaller shapes in the eyes. Then draw some stripe marks which end at the lip line. Add another line between them. Add a pair of circles for the cheeks, and a smaller circle on the chin.

Step 5:

Draw a pole at the bottom of the mask. This will serve as our Puppet's neck.

Step 6:

Remember, he's watching you...

The Secret Animatronic

Okay, so Candy the Cat is just a fan-made animatronic, but she's still super fun to draw!

Step 1:

Circle, then sketch in the facial guidelines.

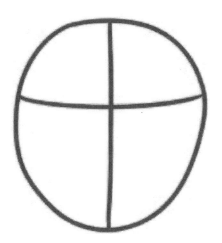

Step 2:

Time to shape the feline's head. Look at how the left and right sides are angled upwards and pointed at the tips.

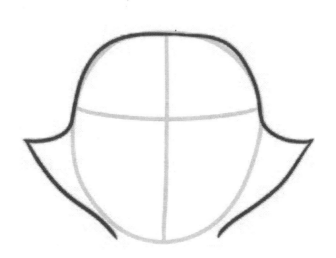

Step 3:

For Candy the Cat's face, draw the inner lining as shown below. Add a pair of circles for the cheeks as well.

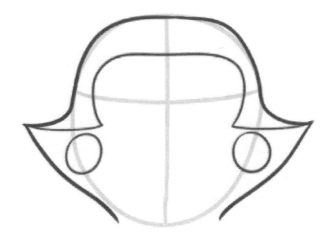

Step 4:

Draw a pair of circles for the eyes, then add the muzzle.

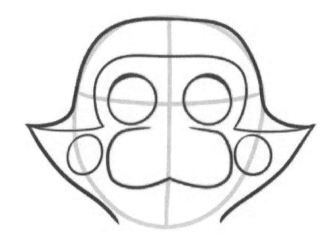

Step 5:

Draw and color in the bananas. Follow that up with a little, triangular nose. Then, add some whisker holes (AKA freckles).

Step 6:

Draw the bottom jaw (which also looks like a banana), then add some mouth lines which connect to the muzzle.

Step 7:

Add a pair of fangs at the top of the mouth and a row of teeth at the bottom. Afterwards, color in the rest of the mouth.

Step 8:

Draw some spear-shaped ears, with smaller spears within them. Connect them to the head with some lines.

Step 9:

Color in the pupils and we're just about finished! To conclude, erase the guidelines, get rid of your mistakes and we're done!

Step 10:

Congratulations! This cute little feline will be haunting your sleep for the next few weeks. Sweet dreams!

Made in the USA
Middletown, DE
19 November 2017